My First Prayer Book

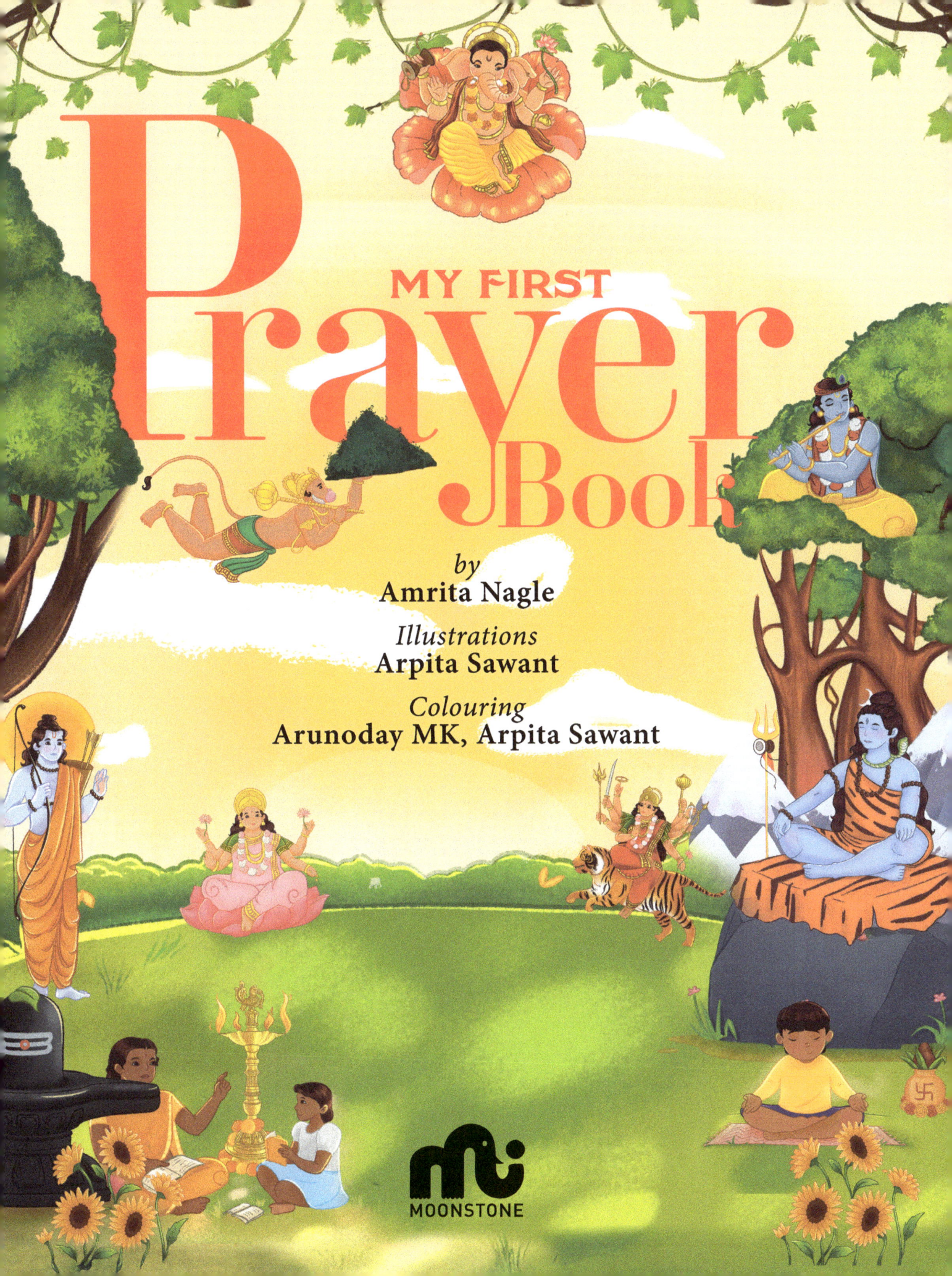

My First Prayer Book

by
Amrita Nagle

Illustrations
Arpita Sawant

Colouring
Arunoday MK, Arpita Sawant

MOONSTONE

Published in Moonstone
by Rupa Publications India Pvt. Ltd 2025
7/16, Ansari Road, Daryaganj
New Delhi 110002

Sales centres:
Bengaluru Chennai
Hyderabad Jaipur Kathmandu
Kolkata Mumbai Prayagraj

Copyright © Amrita Nagle,
Illustrations and colouring by Arpita Sawant and Arunoday MK

All rights reserved.

No part of this publication may be reproduced, transmitted,
or stored in a retrieval system, in any form or by any means,
electronic, mechanical, photocopying, recording or otherwise,
without the prior permission of the publisher.

P-ISBN: 978-93-6156-457-4
E-ISBN: 978-93-6156-985-2

First impression 2025
10 9 8 7 6 5 4 3 2 1

Printed in India
This book is sold subject to the condition that it shall not,
by way of trade or otherwise, be lent, resold, hired out, or otherwise
circulated, without the publisher's prior consent, in any form of binding
or cover other than that in which it is published.

ABOUT THIS BOOK

This book contains 51 Sanskrit shlokas, mantras and subhaashitas.

The verses are written in Devanagari script along with their phonetic transliteration and meaning in English. The book also provides some contextual information about the deities, practices, origin, or significance of each prayer. This additional layer of knowledge helps readers to appreciate the broader context, fostering a sense of curiosity and understanding. The meanings and translations of the verses provided are presented to the best of our knowledge, and we do recognize that the meanings and translations can be subjective, and individuals may interpret the verses differently.

The verses in this book have been put in categories only to better organize the book into sections, but you may realize that many of these prayers or verses belong to two or more categories. The important thing is to understand the meaning and significance of the verse.

The 51 verses in this book are only a tiny drop in the ocean of thousands of shlokas, mantras, prayers and wise sayings from the rich texts we have inherited from our ancestors. We hope this book serves as an introduction to the vast Hindu texts of wisdom and encourages the readers to explore more!

ACKNOWLEDGEMENTS

Heartfelt thanks to Mrs. Aruna Londhe, for her invaluable guidance and expertise in Sanskrit, which has enhanced the authenticity of this book.

Revered gratitude to all the sages, philosophers, scholars, priests and others who contributed to the content of the rich Hindu scriptures, and to the several generations that preserved these over thousands of years, so we could learn from these texts.

Introduction	**page 12**
Devotional	**page 17**
1 - Vakratunda Mahakaya	*pg. 18*
2 - Ya Kundendu	*pg. 20*
3 - Achyutam Keshavam	*pg. 22*
4 - Siddhibuddhiprade Devi	*pg. 24*
5 - Shantakaram Bhujagashayanam	*pg. 26*
6 - Vasudeva Sutam Devam	*pg. 28*
7 - Karpur Gauram Karunavtaram	*pg. 30*
8 - Ramaya Ramabhadraya	*pg. 32*
9 - Mukam Karoti Vachalam	*pg. 34*
Morning	**page 37**
10 - Karagre Vasate Lakshmih	*pg. 38*
11 - Samudravasane Devi	*pg. 40*
12 - Gange Cha Yamune Chaiva	*pg. 42*

TABLE OF CONTENTS

Learning, Art and Music — page 45

    13 - Saraswati Namastubhyam   *pg. 46*
    14 - Gurur Brahma Gurur Vishnu   *pg. 48*
    15 - Nidhaye Sarvavidyanam   *pg. 50*
    16 - Gnanananda Mayam Devam   *pg. 52*
    17 - Namaste Sharade Devi   *pg. 54*
    18 - Aangikam Bhuvanam   *pg. 56*

Everyday — page 59

    19 - Shubham Karoti Kalyanam   *pg. 60*
    20 - Gayatri Mantra   *pg. 62*
    21 - Kayena Vacha   *pg. 64*
    22 - Ya Devi Sarvabhuteshu   *pg. 66*
    23 - Mahamrutyunjaya Mantra   *pg. 68*
    24 - Tvameva Mata   *pg. 70*
    25 - Sarva Mangal Mangalye   *pg. 72*

Mealtime — page 75

    26 - Brahmarpanam Brahma   *pg. 76*
    27 - Annadata Sukhi Bhava   *pg. 78*
    28 - Annapurne Sada Purne   *pg. 80*

Bedtime — page 83

   29 - Ramam Skandam — *pg. 84*
   30 - Buddhirbalam Yasho Dhairyam — *pg. 86*
   31 - Karacharana Krutam — *pg. 88*

Self-Development — page 91

   32 - Karmanyevadhikaraste — *pg. 92*
   33 - Tejo Asi Tejo Mayi — *pg. 94*
   34 - Mitrasya Ma — *pg. 96*
   35 - Udyamena Hi Sidhyanti — *pg. 98*
   36 - Yato Yatah — *pg. 100*
   37 - Vasudhaiva Kutumbakam — *pg. 102*

Nature — page 105

   38 - Namah Suryaya Shantaya — *pg. 106*
   39 - Namah Suryaya Somaya — *pg. 108*
   40 - Chhayamanasya Kurvanti — *pg. 110*

Specific Purpose — page 113

- 41 - Shuklambaradharam Vishnum — *pg. 114*
- 42 - Mangalam Bhagwan Vishnu — *pg. 116*
- 43 - Mahaprasad Janani — *pg. 118*
- 44 - Naivedya Mantra — *pg. 120*

Peace — page 123

- 45 - Om Asato Ma Sadgamaya — *pg. 124*
- 46 - Om Sahana Vavatu — *pg. 126*
- 47 - Kale Varshatu Parjanyah — *pg. 128*
- 48 - Om Sarve Bhavantu Sukhinah — *pg. 130*
- 49 - Om Sarvesham Swastirbhavatu — *pg. 132*
- 50 - Om Purnamadah Purnamidam — *pg. 134*
- 51 - Swasti Prajabhyah — *pg. 136*

Journal and Notes — page 139

INTRODUCTION

What are Hindu Scriptures?

Hindu scriptures are ancient Hindu texts. The composition of these scriptures dates back more than 3,000 years. Hindu scriptures are majorly classified into two categories: Shruti, meaning something that is 'heard' (via meditation or from God), and Smriti, meaning from 'memory' (something that happened and was recorded). These texts are primarily written in the ancient Sanskrit language.

The most prominent scriptures are the four Vedas: the Rigveda, the Yajurveda, the Samaveda, and the Atharvaveda. The word Veda means knowledge in Sanskrit.

These texts are massive and are believed to have had contributions from sages, priests, and philosophers over several hundred years. Each Veda has information in four different sections based on their contents, such as poetic hymns, descriptions of rituals, or philosophical and spiritual subjects. Upanishads are philosophical texts linked to different Vedas. Then there are Vedangas, supporting scriptures that help to understand the Vedas.

Apart from the Vedas, there are also Upavedas, which are scriptures on topics such as medicine, archery, martial arts, music, architecture, and fine arts. The Puranas contain stories about Hindu Gods and Goddesses, kings and sages, and the universe's creation. The Itihasa mainly contains the epics of Ramayana and Mahabharata (including Bhagvad Gita), along with other works. The Shad-Darshan is a set of six philosophical works written by sages. One of these is Yog Darshan by Sage Patanjali, which describes yoga practice.

Apart from those mentioned here, there are numerous other texts, too many to list here. Hindu scriptures are thus a vast treasure of knowledge that can help all of us learn, grow, and become wiser.

A majority of the verses and prayers in this book originate from these Hindu scriptures.

Why do we learn these mantras, shlokas and other verses?

This book contains 51 Sanskrit verses, that include *shlokas, mantras, subhaashitas,* and other types of verses. Some benefits of the practice of learning and reciting these ancient verses are given below.

- It helps establish a spiritual connection and relationship with the divine.

- These verses are an integral part of Hindu culture and tradition. This is a way of preserving and passing on ancient wisdom to future generations.

- It relieves restlessness and anxiety, as well as calms the mind. Rhythmic chanting also improves breathing patterns.

- Chanting is believed to improve cognitive function. Cognitive function encompasses mental abilities such as thinking, learning, problem solving, reasoning, memory, and attention.

- Vocalising these Sanskrit verses improves pronunciation, speech, and language.

- By expressing our gratitude and respect towards the earth, sun, nature, teachers, parents, and more, these verses teach us to be grateful and humble.

In essence, learning and reciting these verses promotes spiritual devotion, cultural preservation, mental focus, and overall well-being. It is a tool that can improve our connection with the divine, help us deal with life's challenges, and cultivate a sense of harmony.

An audio of all prayers and verses in this book is available on the YouTube channel :

'Hindu Prayers for Kids'

https://youtube.com/@hinduprayersforkids-w5w?si=c-LitK01aM_r_QXL

DEVOTIONAL

Vakratunda Mahakaya

वक्रतुण्ड महाकाय सूर्यकोटि समप्रभ ।
निर्विघ्नं कुरु मे देव सर्वकार्येषु सर्वदा ॥

· Transliteration ·

Vakratunda Mahaakaaya Suryakoti Samaprabha |
Nirvighnam Kuru Me Deva Sarvakaaryeshu Sarvadaa ||

· Meaning ·

The one with a curved trunk and majestic body (Ganesha), whose brilliance is equivalent to billions of suns. Bless me and remove obstacles from all my endeavours.

· Information ·

Lord Ganesha is the God of prosperity, wisdom and is known as the remover of all obstacles. Ganesha is worshipped before starting anything new, as He is believed to bring good luck, success and prosperity. This prayer can be recited before starting a new task or activity, and even every day, especially in the morning.

Ya Kundendu

या कुन्देन्दुतुषारहारधवला या शुभ्रवस्त्रावृता
या वीणावरदण्डमण्डितकरा या श्वेतपद्मासना ।
या ब्रह्माच्युत शङ्करप्रभृतिभिर्देवैः सदा वन्दिता
सा मां पातु सरस्वती भगवती निःशेषजाड्यापहा ॥

• Transliteration •

Yaa Kundendutushaarahaaradhavalaa Yaa Shubhravastraavrutaa
Yaa Veenaavaradandamanditakaraa Yaa Shvetapadmaasanaa |
Yaa Brahmaachyuta Shankaraprabhrutibhirdevaih Sadaa Vanditaa
Saa Maam Paatu Saraswati Bhagavati Nihsheshajaadyapahaa ||

• Meaning •

The one who is white like jasmine flowers, like the moon, like snow and a pearl necklace, who is dressed in pure white clothes, whose hands are adorned with a veena, who sits on a white lotus, who is always worshipped by Brahma, Vishnu, Shankara and other Gods; Goddess Saraswati, please take care of me and eliminate my ignorance.

• Information •

Saraswati vandana is a part of the Saraswati stotram written by Sage Agastya and occurs in the Rig Veda. Saraswati is the Goddess of knowledge, art, music, learning and wisdom. This Vandana can be recited before studies or practicing music or any form of art to seek the Goddess' blessings.

Achyutam Keshavam

अच्युतं केशवं रामनारायणं
कृष्णदामोदरं वासुदेवं हरिम् ।
श्रीधरं माधवं गोपिकावल्लभं
जानकीनायकं रामचंद्रं भजे ॥

Transliteration

Achyutam Keshavam Raamanaaraayanam
Krushnadaamodaram Vaasudevam Harim |
Shridharam Maadhavam Gopikaavallabham
Jaanakinaayakam Raamachandram Bhaje ||

Meaning

I worship You in the forms of Achyuta, Keshava, Rama, the incarnation of Narayana, Krishna-also known as Damodara, son of Vasudeva, and Hari. I worship you in forms of Shridhara, Madhava, the beloved of all Gopikas, and Rama, the Lord of Goddess Janaki.

Information

These lines form the first verse of the "Achyutashtakam", a hymn dedicated to Lord Krishna, composed by Adi Shankaracharya. It consists of eight verses that highlight various divine attributes and forms of Krishna.

Siddhibuddhiprade Devi

सिद्धिबुद्धिप्रदे देवि भुक्तिमुक्तिप्रदायिनि ।
मन्त्रमूर्ते सदा देवि महालक्ष्मि नमोऽस्तुते ॥

Transliteration

Siddhibuddhiprade Devi Bhuktimuktipradaayini |
Mantramurte Sadaa Devi Mahaalakshmi Namo-stute ||

Meaning

Goddess Mahalakshmi, who bestows success and intellect, wordly prosperity and liberation. Who always abides as an embodiment of mantras, I bow down to you.

Information

The name 'Lakshmi' is derived from the Sanskrit word Lakshya meaning goal. Goddess Lakshmi's blessings can help you reach your goals. This prayer is a part of Mahalakshmi Ashtakam, found in Padma Purana, and is said to have been composed by Lord Indra.

Shantakaram Bhujagashayanam

शान्ताकारं भुजगशयनं पद्मनाभं सुरेशं
विश्वाधारं गगनसदृशं मेघवर्णं शुभाङ्गम् ।
लक्ष्मीकान्तं कमलनयनं योगिभिर्ध्यानगम्यं
वन्दे विष्णुं भवभयहरं सर्वलोकैकनाथम् ॥

Transliteration

Shaantaakaaram Bhujagashayanam Padmanaabham Suresham
Vishvaadhaaram Gaganasadrusham Meghavarnam Shubhaangam |
Lakshmikaantam Kamalanayanam Yogibhirdhyaanagamyam
Vande Vishnum Bhavabhayaharam Sarvalokaekanaatham ||

Meaning

I offer my prayers to Lord Vishnu, the one who has a tranquil appearance, who rests on a serpent, who has a lotus on his navel, who is the Lord of all Gods. He is the sustainer of the universe, boundless like the sky, his colour is like that of the clouds, and has an auspicious body. The beloved of Goddess Lakshmi, the lotus-eyed one, who is meditated upon by the Yogis. I bow down to Shri Vishnu, the remover of fear and the Lord of all worlds.

Information

This shloka expresses devotion and admiration for Lord Vishnu. It is a part of the dhyana shlokas in the Vishnu Sahasranaama, which is a part of the epic Mahaabharata.

Vasudeva Sutam Devam

वसुदेवसुतं देवं कंसचाणूरमर्दनम् ।
देवकीपरमानन्दं कृष्णं वंदे जगद्गुरुम् ॥

• **Transliteration** •

Vasudevasutam Devam Kamsachaanurmardanam |
Devakiparamaanandam Krushnam Vande Jagadgurum ||

• **Meaning** •

I bow to Lord Krishna, who is the Guru of the universe, the son of Vasudeva, destroyer of the evil Kamsa and Chanura, and the bliss of mother Devaki.

• **Information** •

This is one of the eight verses dedicated to Krishna in Krushnaashtakam. All verses end with the phrase meaning "I bow to Krishna, the Guru of the universe".

Karpur Gauram Karunavtaram

कर्पूरगौरं करुणावतारं
संसारसारं भुजगेन्द्रहारम् ।
सदावसन्तं हृदयारविन्दे
भवं भवानीसहितं नमामि ॥

Transliteration

Karpurgauram Karunaavataaram
Samsaarsaaram Bhujagendrahaaram |
Sadaavasantam Hrudayaaravinde
Bhavam Bhavaanisahitam Namaami ||

Meaning

I pray to Lord Shiva who is radiant as camphor, kind and compassionate, the essence of the entire universe. Who wears a serpent as a garland, resides in hearts pure as the lotus flower, I bow to Him together with Goddess Bhavani (Parvati).

Information

This is a devotional mantra found in Yajurveda that praises Lord Shiva's qualities, compassion, and transcendental nature.

Ramaya Ramabhadraya

रामाय रामभद्राय रामचन्द्राय वेधसे ।
रघुनाथाय नाथाय सितायाः पतये नमः ॥

• Transliteration •

Raamaaya Raamabhadraaya Raamchandraaya Vedhase |
Raghunaathaaya Naathaaya Sitaayaah Pataye Namah ||

• Meaning •

Shri Rama, who is also known as Ramabhadra and Ramachandra, who is all-knowledgeable. He is the greatest of the kings of Raghu clan, the Lord of all, the consort of Goddess Sita, I bow down to Him.

• Information •

Lord Rama is the seventh avatar of Vishnu, and a main character in the epic Ramayana. This shloka describes Lord Rama using his different names and qualities. It acknowledges Rama's auspiciousness, His connection with Sita, Him as a king of the Raghu dynasty, and as the Lord of lords.

Mukam Karoti Vachalam

मूकं करोति वाचालं पङ्गुं लङ्घयते गिरिम् |
यत्कृपा तमहं वन्दे परमानन्द माधवम् ॥

• Transliteration •

Mukam Karoti Vaachaalam Pangum Langhayate Girim |
Yatkrupaa Tamaham Vande Paramaanandam Maadhavam ||

• Meaning •

I offer my prayers to Madhava (Shri Krishna), who is the supreme joy. His grace can make the voiceless speak and empower the crippled to cross mountains.

• Information •

This shloka describes the grace and mercy of Lord Krishna, who is the eighth incarnation of Vishnu. Krishna represents love, kindness and joy. Many devotees consider Krishna as a friend, companion, and protector, who can guide us to the right path.

MORNING

Karagre Vasate Lakshmih

कराग्रे वसते लक्ष्मीः करमध्ये सरस्वती ।
करमूले तु गोविन्दः प्रभाते करदर्शनम् ॥

• Transliteration •

Karaagre Vasate Lakshmih Karamadhye Saraswati |
Karamoole Tu Govindah Prabhaate Karadarshanam||

• Meaning •

Lakshmi resides at the tips of hands, Saraswati in the middle, and Govinda (Krishna) at the base of our hands. We look at our hands every morning and contemplate on them.

• Information •

Recite this mantra as soon as you get up, before getting down from the bed. Focus your attention on the tips, centre and base of your hands as you recite it and gently swipe the hands over your face. Your hands do all the tasks for you, take a moment to reflect on them before starting your day.

समुद्रवसने देवि पर्वतस्तनमण्डले ।
विष्णुपत्नि नमस्तुभ्यं पादस्पर्शं क्षमस्वमे ॥

· Transliteration ·

Samudravasane Devi Parvatastanamandale |
Vishnupatni Namastubhyam Paadasparsham Kshamasvame ||

· Meaning ·

I bow down to you Mother Earth, who has the oceans as garments, mountains as bosom and who is the wife of Vishnu (Varaha avatar). I seek your forgiveness as I put my feet on you.

· Information ·

Mother Earth is shown as Bhoomi Devi in Hindu mythology. This prayer is recited every morning, before stepping on the floor, to ask Bhoomi Devi for forgiveness for stepping on her. Mother Earth nourishes and sustains all of us, and it is our duty to respect, protect and take care of Her.

Gange Cha Yamune Chaiva

गङ्गे च यमुने चैव गोदावरी सरस्वती ।
नर्मदे सिन्धु कावेरी जलेऽस्मिन् सन्निधिं कुरु ॥

• Transliteration •

Gange Cha Yamune Chaiva Godaavari Saraswati |
Narmade Sindhu Kaaveri Jale-smin Sannidhim Kuru ||

• Meaning •

May the holy rivers Ganga, Yamuna, Godavari, Saraswati, Narmada, Sindhu, Kaveri come together and establish their auspicious presence in this water.

• Information •

Waters of the holy rivers of India are considered to purify you when you bathe in them. By reciting this shloka before bathing, you invoke the presence of the sacred rivers in your bath water such that it purifies your body and mind. The picture shows river Ganga as a Goddess.

LEARNING, ART & MUSIC

Saraswati Namastubhyam

सरस्वती नमस्तुभ्यं वरदे कामरूपिणि ।
विद्यारम्भं करिष्यामि सिद्धिर्भवतु मे सदा ॥

• Transliteration •

Saraswati Namastubhyam Varade Kaamrupini |
Vidyaarambham Karishyaami Siddhirbhavatu Me Sadaa ||

• Meaning •

I bow down to you, Goddess Saraswati, the one who grants blessings and embodies all my wishes. Bless me with the wisdom to be successful as I begin my studies.

• Information •

Students chant this shloka before starting studies or any learning activities, to seek blessings of Goddess Saraswati for knowledge, wisdom and success.

Gurur Brahma Gurur Vishnu

गुरुर्ब्रह्मा गुरुर्विष्णुः गुरुर्देवो महेश्वरः ।
गुरुः साक्षात् परं ब्रह्म तस्मै श्री गुरवे नमः ॥

Transliteration

Gurur Brahmaa Gurur Vishnuh Gurur Devo Maheshwarah |
Guruh Saakshaat Param Brahma Tasmai Shri Guruve Namah ||

Meaning

Guru, you are Brahma, you are Vishnu, you are Maheshwara (Shiva). Guru, you are the supreme God, my salutations to you.

Information

Guru vandana is a way of expressing gratitude and respect to the teacher. The Guru or teacher is equated to God. The word "Guru" means remover of darkness (ignorance), as through their teachings Gurus spread knowledge and enlighten us.

Nidhaye Sarvavidyanam

50

निधये सर्वविद्यानां भिषजे भवरोगिणाम् ।
गुरवे सर्वलोकानां दक्षिणामूर्तये नमः ॥

Transliteration

Nidhaye Sarvavidyaanaam Bhishaje Bhavroginaam |
Gurave Sarvalokaanaam Dakshinaamurtaye Namah ||

Meaning

I pray to Lord Dakshinamurti who is the reservoir of knowledge, healer of the disease of worldly attachments, and teacher of the entire world.

Information

Lord Dakshinamurti is an avatar of Shiva, and is considered to be the supreme Guru, embodiment of knowledge and the destroyer of ignorance.

Gnanananda Mayam Devam

ज्ञानानन्दमयं देवं निर्मल स्फटिकाकृतिम् ।
आधारं सर्व विद्द्यानां हयग्रीवं उपास्महे ॥

• Transliteration •

Gnaanaanandamayam Devam Nirmala Sphatikaakrutim |
Aadharam Sarvavidyaanaam Hayagreevam Upaasmahe ||

• Meaning •

I worship Lord Hayagreeva, who is the embodiment of knowledge and bliss, pure as a crystal, and the foundation of all knowledge.

• Information •

Lord Hayagreeva, an avatar of Vishnu, is the God of knowledge and wisdom. He is believed to bestow devotees with knowledge, clarity of thought, good memory and mastery over speech.

Namaste Sharade Devi

नमस्ते शारदे देवि काश्मीरपुरवासिनि ।
त्वामहं प्रार्थये नित्यं विद्यां बुद्धिं च देहि मे ॥

• Transliteration •

Namaste Shaarade Devi Kaashmirpurvaasini |
Tvaamaham Praarthaye Nityam Vidyaam Buddhim Cha Dehi Me ||

• Meaning •

Goddess Sharada, who lives in Kashmir, I pray to you everyday to bless me with knowledge and intellect.

• Information •

This is another shloka invoking the blessings of Goddess Sharada, another name for Saraswati, the Goddess of learning and knowledge.

Aangikam Bhuvanam

आङ्गिकं भुवनं यस्य
वाचिकं सर्व वाङ्ग्मयम् ।
आहार्यं चन्द्रतारादि
तं नमः सात्विकं शिवम् ॥

• Transliteration •

Aangikam Bhuvanam Yasya
Vaachikam Sarva Vaangmayam |
Aahaaryam Chandra Taaraadi
Tam Namah Saatvikam Shivam ||

• Meaning •

We bow to Lord Shiva, whose body is the whole universe, whose speech is all of the world's languages and whose body is adorned with the moon and stars.

• Information •

Nataraja is a form of Lord Shiva and is known as the 'Lord of dance.' This shloka is recited by dancers when they start their dance practice to seek blessings of Lord Shiva or Nataraja.

EVERYDAY

Shubham Karoti Kalyanam

शुभं करोति कल्याणं आरोग्यं धनसंपदा ।
शत्रुबुद्धि विनाशाय दीपज्योतिर्नमोऽस्तुते ॥

· Transliteration ·

Shubham Karoti Kalyaanam Aarogyam Dhanasampadaa |
Shatrubuddhi Vinaashaaya Deepajyotirnamo-stute ||

· Meaning ·

Salutations to the light of the lamp, from where arises all auspiciousness, health and prosperity, and that destroys bad feelings (like anger, jealousy, and greed).

· Information ·

All pujas and auspicious rituals begin with lighting the lamp. This shloka is for the light of the lamp, which eliminates darkness. Light signifies knowledge or enlightenment, whereas darkness represents ignorance or evil. This can be recited while lighting the lamp during daily prayers or any rituals.

Gayatri Mantra

ॐ भूर्भुवः स्वः तत्सवितुर्वरेण्यं
भर्गोदेवस्य धीमहि धियो यो नः प्रचोदयात् ॥

Transliteration

Om Bhurbhuvah Swaha Tatsaviturvarenyam
Bhargodevasya Dhimahi Dhiyo Yo Nah Prachodayaat ||

Meaning

Oh creator of the universe, we meditate upon your glory. May your radiance illuminate our intellects, destroy our ignorance and enlighten us.

Information

Gayatri mantra appears in the Rigveda and is one of the oldest and most familiar Sanskrit mantras. The mantra is dedicated to God Savitr (सवितृ), a form of Sun God, and is written in the Gayatri meter. Goddess Gayatri, a personification of this mantra, is considered as the mother of the Vedas. This is a powerful mantra that can be chanted in the morning and evening to improve concentration, remove negative feelings and to bring upon peace and happiness.

Kayena Vacha

कायेन वाचा मनसेन्द्रियैर्वा
बुद्ध्यात्मना वा प्रकृतिस्वभावात् ।
करोमि यद्यत्सकलं परस्मै
नारायणयेति समर्पयामि ॥

Transliteration

Kaayena Vaachaa Manasaeindriyairvaa
Buddhyaatmanaa Vaa Prakrutisvabhaavat |
Karomi Yadyatsakalam Parasmai
Naaraayanayeti Samarpayaami ||

Meaning

Whatever I do with my body, speech, mind or my senses, either by my intellect, or from the heart, or from the natural instincts of my mind, I do them all without attachment, and I surrender them at the feet of God Narayana (Vishnu).

Information

This shloka for Lord Vishnu encourages us to be humble and selfless. Vishnu is "Preserver" of the Hindu trinity of Gods, along with Brahma the "Creator" and Shiva the "Destroyer". Vishnu has ten avatars or incarnations, including Rama and Krishna.

Ya Devi Sarvabhuteshu

या देवी सर्वभूतेषु बुद्धिरूपेण संस्थिता ।
नमस्तस्यै नमस्तस्यै नमस्तस्यै नमो नमः ॥
या देवी सर्वभूतेषु शक्तिरूपेण संस्थिता ।
नमस्तस्यै नमस्तस्यै नमस्तस्यै नमो नमः ॥

· Transliteration ·

Yaa Devi Sarvabhuteshu Buddhirupena Samsthitaa |
Namastasyai Namastasyai Namastasyai Namo Namah ||
Yaa Devi Sarvabhuteshu Shaktirupena Samsthitaa |
Namastasyai Namastasyai Namastasyai Namo Namah ||

· Meaning ·

I offer my salutations again and again to the Goddess
who lives in all beings in the form of intelligence.
I offer my salutations again and again to the Goddess
who lives in all beings in the form of strength.

· Information ·

These verses are a part of the Devi Stuti that occurs in
the Devi Mahatmyam - a text describing Goddess Durga in
700 verses. The stuti highlights how the Goddess or
Divine Mother is omnipresent, she is present in
everything and at all times.

ॐ त्र्यम्बकं यजामहे
सुगन्धिं पुष्टिवर्धनम् ।
उर्वारुकमिव बन्धनान्
मृत्योर्मुक्षीयमामृतात् ॥

• Transliteration •

Om Tryambakam Yajaamahe
Sugandhim Pushtivardhanam |
Urvarukamiva Bandhanaan
Mrutyormukshiyamaamrutaat ||

• Meaning •

We worship the three-eyed God (Shiva), who radiates like a fragrance that nourishes us. May we be liberated from the bondage of death for the sake of immortality, like a fruit is freed from its tree.

• Information •

The Mahamrutyunjaya mantra is considered to be one of the most powerful mantras from Rigveda that can help to calm the mind and can be chanted to seek good health for self or others. This prayer dedicated to Lord Shiva is usually chanted early in the morning, but can be chanted anytime during the day or before going to bed.

त्वमेव माता च पिता त्वमेव ।
त्वमेव बन्धुश्च सखा त्वमेव ।
त्वमेव विद्या द्रविणं त्वमेव ।
त्वमेव सर्वं मम देव देव ॥

• Transliteration •

Tvameva Maataa Cha Pitaa Tvameva |
Tvameva Bandhushcha Sakhaa Tvameva ||
Tvameva Vidyaa Dravinam Tvameva |
Tvameva Sarvam Mama Deva Deva ||

• Meaning •

You are my mother and my father, you are my family and my friend, you are my knowledge and my wealth, my God of Gods, you are everything to me.

• Information •

These verses occur in Pandava Gita, a hymn containing several verses dedicated to Lord Krishna or Lord Vishnu. This verse is said to have been recited by Gandhari, the mother of Kauravas, to Shri Krishna. This simple shloka encourages us to surrender to God and can be chanted during daily prayers.

Sarva Mangal Mangalye

सर्वमङ्गलमाङ्गल्ये शिवे सर्वार्थसाधिके ।
शरण्ये त्र्यम्बके गौरि नारायणि नमोऽस्तुते ॥

• Transliteration •

Sarvamangalmaangalye Shive Sarvaarthasaadhike |
Sharanye Tryambake Gauri Naaraayani Namo-stute ||

• Meaning •

Goddess Narayani, who is the auspiciousness of all that is auspicious, the consort of Lord Shiva, the means of fulfilling wishes, the refuge for all, the three-eyed one, I bow down to you.

• Information •

According to a popular legend, Brahma, Vishnu and Shiva created Goddess Durga to slay the demon Mahishasura. She is a powerful Goddess who protects us as a mother and destroys all evil. This prayer is a part of the Devi Mahatmyam.

MEALTIME

Brahmarpanam Brahma

ब्रह्मार्पणं ब्रह्म हविर्ब्रह्माग्नौ ब्रह्मणा हुतम् ।
ब्रह्मैव तेन गन्तव्यं ब्रह्मकर्मसमाधिना ॥

• Transliteration •

Brahmaarpanam Brahma Havirbrahmaagnau Brahmanaa Hutam |
Brahmaiva Tena Gantavyam Brahamakarmasamaadhina ||

• Meaning •

The act of offering is Brahman (supreme divinity), the offering (food) itself is Brahman. The fire into which it is offered (our digestive system) is Brahman and the one who is offering is also Brahman. The one who is fully absorbed in Brahman, in all their actions, will only attain Brahman. (Brahman is the supreme divinity, the infinite soul of the universe or the ultimate consciousness).

• Information •

We often eat food in a hurry, eating while looking at our screens and paying little attention to what we are eating. Reciting this mantra allows us to reflect and think about the food and how it will nourish not only our body but our mind too.
Some similar terms with different meanings:

Brahman = ब्रह्मन् (or ब्रह्म) = supreme divinity,

ultimate conciousness. Brahmaa = ब्रह्मा = God Brahma, the creator

Braahmana = ब्राह्मण = one of the four classes of the socitey - the scholar or philosopher (based on their qualities and deeds).

अन्नदाता सुखी भव ।

• Transliteration •

Annadaataa Sukhi Bhava |

• Meaning •

May the provider of this food be happy.

• Information •

This is a simple phrase of gratitude for the provider of your food. The provider could be the person who cooked the food, the farmer who grew the food, the shopkeeper or grocer who sourced it, the person who served or delivered it or the natural elements that helped it grow.

Annapurne Sada Purne

अन्नपूर्णे सदा पूर्णे शङ्करप्राणवल्लभे ।
ज्ञानवैराग्यसिद्ध्यर्थं भिक्षां देहि च पार्वति ॥

Transliteration

Annapurne Sadaa Purne Shankarapraanvallabhe |
Gnaanvairaagyasidhyartham Bhikshaam Dehi Cha Paarvati ||

Meaning

Goddess Annapurna, you are always bountiful with food and blessings. You are the consort of Lord Shankara (Shiva). Bless me with good health, wisdom and detachment (from worldly desires), Goddess Parvati.

Information

Annapurna is the Goddess of food and nourishment, and is a form of Goddess Parvati. Anna means food and purna means complete or full. She holds a bowl of food in one hand and a ladle in the other. This verse is a part of the Annapurna stotram.

BEDTIME

Ramam Skandam

रामं स्कन्दं हनूमन्तं वैनतेयं वृकोदरम् ।
शयने यः स्मरेन्नित्यं दुःस्वप्नस्तस्य नश्यति ॥

Transliteration

Raamam Skandam Hanumantam Vainateyam Vrukodaram |
Shayane Yah Smarennityam Dusvapnastasya Nashyati ||

Meaning

Keeping good thoughts of the courageous Shri Rama,
Kartikeya, Hanuman, Garuda and Bheema in our minds
before going to sleep every night prevents us
from having nightmares.

Information

Lord Rama, Lord Kartikeya, Lord Hanuman,
Garuda and Bheema represent strength and bravery.
Having them in our thoughts would give us courage too and
drive away the negative thoughts that cause nightmares.

Buddhirbalam Yasho Dhairyam

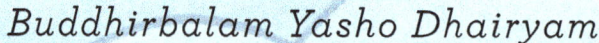

बुद्धिर्बलं यशो धैर्यं निर्भयत्वमरोगिता ।
अजाड्यं वाक्पटुत्वं च हनूमत्स्मरणाद्भवेत् ॥

· Transliteration ·

Buddhirbalam Yasho Dhairyam Nirbhayatvamarogitaa |
Ajaadyam Vaakpatutvam Cha Hanumatsmaranaadbhavet ||

· Meaning ·

Intelligence, strength, success, bravery, fearlessness, good health, sharp wit, eloquence and diplomacy - all these will be attained by meditating on Shri Hanuman.

· Information ·

Lord Hanuman is simple and kind, yet very strong and brave. Thinking about his qualities makes one courageous and fearless. Although this prayer can be recited at anytime, contemplating on Hanuman before bedtime can help us get rid of our fears and have a peaceful sleep.

करचरण कृतं वाक्कायजं कर्मजं वा
श्रवणनयनजं वा मानसं वापराधम् ।
विहितमविहितं वा सर्वमेतत्क्षमस्व
जय जय करुणाब्धे श्रीमहादेव शम्भो ॥

• Transliteration •

Karacharana Krutam Vaakkaayajam Karmajam Vaa
Shravananayanajam Vaa Maanasam Vaaparaadham |
Vihitamavihitam Vaa Sarvametatkshamasva
Jaya Jaya Karunaabdhe Shrimahaadeva Shambho ||

• Meaning •

I seek forgiveness for any wrongdoings I may have committed, with my hands, feet, words, ears, eyes, or mind, knowingly or unknowingly. Forgive me Lord Mahadeva (Shiva), who is the ocean of kindness and compassion.

• Information •

This prayer is to seek forgiveness from Lord Shiva for any mistakes or wrongdoings we may have committed. It can be earnestly recited the end of day before going to sleep.

SELF-DEVELOPMENT

Karmanyevadhikaraste

कर्मण्येवाधिकारस्ते मा फलेषु कदाचन ।
मा कर्मफलहेतुर्भुर्मा ते संगोऽस्त्वकर्मणि ॥

• Transliteration •

Karmanyevaadhikaaraste Maa Phaleshu Kadaachana |
Maa Karmaphalaheturbhurmaa Te Sango-stvakarmani ||

• Meaning •

You are only entitled to do your work but not to its 'fruit' or outcome. Do not let the expectation of the 'fruit' (or outcome) of your work be your motivation, and do not be attached to inaction.

• Information •

This is one of the most well-known shlokas from the Bhagavad Gita, a text that presents a conversation between Arjuna and his charioteer and guide, Krishna, during the battle of Mahabharata. Although the setting of the converstaion was very different, Krishna's advice to Arjuna can be aptly applied to our lives today.

Tejo Asi Tejo Mayi

तेजो ऽसि तेजो मयि देहि । वीर्यम् असि वीर्यं मयि देहि ।
बलम् असि बलं मयि देहि । ओजो ऽसि ओजो मयि देहि ।
मन्युर् असि मन्युं मयि देहि । सहो ऽसि सहो मयि देहि ॥

Transliteration

Tejo Asi Tejo Mayi Dehi | Viryam Asi Viryam Mayi Dehi |
Balam Asi Balam Mayi Dehi | Ojo Asi Ojo Mayi Dehi |
Manyur Asi Manyum Mayi Dehi | Saho Asi Saho Mayi Dehi ||

Meaning

You are the radiance, bless me to make me radiant, you are the courage, bless me to make me courageous, you are the strength, bless me to make me strong, you are the vigour, bless me with your vigour, you are fierce, bless me to make me brave, you are the patience, bless me to make me patient .

Information

This prayer does not ask for material things, but prays for good qualities in onself. This can be addressed to any deity, nature or the universe.

Mitrasya Ma

मित्रस्य मा चक्षुषा सर्वाणि भूतानि समीक्षन्ताम् ।
मित्रस्याहं चक्षुषा सर्वाणि भूतानि समीक्षे मित्रस्य चक्षुषा समीक्षामहे ॥

Transliteration

Mitrasya Maa Chakshushaa Sarvaani Bhutaani Samikshantaam |
Mitrasyaaham Chakshushaa Sarvaani Bhutaani Samikshe
Mitrasya Chakshushaa Samikshaamahe ||

Meaning

May nature and all its living beings see me with a friendly eye and may I look at nature and all its living beings with a friendly eye. Let us all see each other in a friendly way and live harmoniously.

Information

This Subhashita urges us to live in harmony with not only other people, but also with animals, plants, and other natural elements. Inculcating these values is among the first steps we can take as individuals towards world peace and protecting our environment.

Udyamena Hi Siddyanti

उद्यमेन हि सिध्यन्ति कार्याणि न मनोरथैः ।
न हि सुप्तस्य सिंहस्य प्रविशन्ति मुखे मृगाः ॥

• Transliteration •

Udyamena Hi Sidhyanti Kaaryaani Na Manorathyaih |
Na Hi Suptasya Simhasya Pravishanti Mukhe Mrugaah ||

• Meaning •

Just as a deer does not enter the mouth of a sleeping lion, tasks cannot be accomplished merely by thinking about them. Only hardwork can help one achieve success.

• Information •

It is great to have good thoughts and ideas, but to achieve something you also have to put your thoughts into action. Hardwork is essential to reach your goals.

Yato Yatah

यतो यतः समीहसे ततो नोऽभयं कुरु ।
शन्नः कुरु प्रजाभ्योऽभयं नः पशुभ्यः ॥

· Transliteration ·

Yato Yatah Samihase Tato No-abhayam Kuru |
Shannah Kuru Prajaabhyo-bhayam Nah Pashubhyah ||

· Meaning ·

Whatever manner you approach us, make us fearless from them all. Make us feel safe. May all people and animals be safe without fear.

· Information ·

This is often recited as a prayer for protection and safety, seeking the divine's protection for oneself and the community from any harm or adversity.

Vasudhaiva Kutumbakam

अयं निजः परो वेति गणना लघुचेतसाम्।
उदारचरितानां तु वसुधैव कुटुम्बकम्॥

Transliteration

Ayam Nijah Paro Veti Gananaa Laghuchetsaam
Udaarcharitaanaam Tu Vasudhaiva Kutumbakam ||

Meaning

This person is a friend, while that one is an outlander,
say the narrow-minded.
For the wise, the entire world is a family.

Information

The ancient idea of "entire world is a family" encourages us to look beyond each other's differences and accept everyone as our own. The phrase "Vasudhaiva Kutumbakam" from this subhashita has even been used by Indian government to promote peace and brotherhood.

NATURE

नमः सूर्याय शान्ताय सर्वरोग निवारिणे
आयुरारोग्यम् ऐश्वर्यं देहि देवः जगत्पते ॥

• Transliteration •

Namah Suryaaya Shaantaaya Sarvaroga Nivaarine
Aayuraarogyam Aishvaryam Dehi Devah Jagatpate ||

• Meaning •

I bow down to Lord Surya, who is the ruler of the universe,
the restorer of peace and remover of all diseases.
May He bless us with a long life, good health and prosperity.

• Information •

The Sun God also known as Surya in Hinduism, is the source of all life forms and energy on earth. Sun gives us light and warmth, without which no life would be possible on earth. He rides a chariot driven by seven horses named after the seven meters used in Sanskrit literature. The seven horses can also be attributed to seven colours that form the sunlight.

Namah Suryaya Somaya

नमः सूर्याय सोमाय मङ्गळाय बुधाय च |
गुरु शुक्र शनिभ्यश्च राहवे केतवे नमः ॥

· Transliteration ·

Namah Suryaaya Somaaya Mangalaaya Budhaaya Cha |
Guru Shukra Shanibhyascha Raahave Ketave Namah ||

· Meaning ·

My salutations to the Sun, to the Moon, and to the
planets Mars, Mercury, Jupiter, Venus, Saturn, Raahu and Ketu.

· Information ·

Based on astrology, planetary positions are believed to
have a great impact on our life. By chanting this mantra,
we offer our prayers to the "navagraha" or nine planets
to liberate us from the ill effects due to planetary positions.

Chhayamanasya Kurvanti

छायामन्यस्य कुर्वन्ति तिष्ठन्ति स्वयमातपे।
फलान्यापि परार्थाय वृक्षाः सत्पुरुषा इव॥

· Transliteration ·

Chhayamanasya Kurvanti Tishthanti Swayamaatpe |
Phalaanyaapi Paraarthaaya Vrukshaah Satpurshaa Iva ||

· Meaning ·

They stand in the sun while giving others shade.
Their fruits are also for others. Trees are (selfless)
like good people.

· Information ·

Trees and plants are the sustainers of earth. It is our duty to protect trees by adopting environmental friendly habits and lifestyles. As you read this subhashita, take some time to reflect on how our lives depend on plants and trees; from the oxygen we breathe to the food we eat to the paper we write on, as a shelter for animals, their effect on the climate, and many more.

SPECIFIC PURPOSE

Shuklambaradharam Vishnum

शुक्लाम्बरधरं विष्णुं शशिवर्णं चतुर्भुजम् ।
प्रसन्नवदनं ध्यायेत् सर्वविघ्नोपशान्तये ॥

Transliteration

Shuklaambaradharam Vishnum Shashivarnam Chaturbhujam |
Prasannavadanam Dhyaayet Sarvavighnopshaantaye ||

Meaning

The One who is wearing white clothing, who is all-pervasive, who is bright like the moon, who has four arms and a cheerful face; we meditate on Him to remove all obstacles.

Information

A popular prayer to overcome vighna or obstacles that may prevent you from achieving your goals. This is often recited before starting a new task. Some people address to this to Lord Ganesha, some to Lord Vishnu and others to Vishvaksena, the commander of Lord Vishnu's army. You can meditate upon the deity you believe in, when reciting this shloka.

Mangalam Bhagwan Vishnu

मङ्गलं भगवान विष्णुः मङ्गलं गरुडध्वजः ।
मङ्गलं पुण्डरी काक्षः मङ्गलाय तनो हरिः ॥

Transliteration

Mangalam Bhagwaan Vishnuh Mangalam Garudadhwajah |
Mangalam Pundari Kaakshah Mangalaaya Tano Harih ||

Meaning

All auspiciousness to Lord Vishnu, all auspiciousness
to the one who has Garuda on his flag.
All auspiciousness to the Lord who has eyes like the lotus flower,
and all auspiciousness to Hari (an avatar of Vishnu).

Information

This mantra is recited before any auspicious tasks
or rituals like wedding, pujas, aartis, and others.
Reciting this mantra is believed to bring good luck, health,
happiness, prosperity and success.

Mahaprasad Janani

महाप्रसाद जननी सर्व सौभाग्यवर्धिनी ।
आधि व्याधि हरा नित्यं तुलसी त्वं नमोऽस्तुते ॥

· Transliteration ·

Mahaaprasaad Janani Sarva Saubhaagyavardhini |
Aadhi Vyaadhi Haraa Nityam Tulsi Twam Namo-stute ||

· Meaning ·

We pray to you Goddess Tulsi, who blesses everyone with good fortune, destroys diseases of the mind and body and keeps us healthy.

· Information ·

Tulsi is one of the most sacred plants in Hinduism. Tulsi is also known as Vrinda, and the plant is known to have several medicinal properties. Chant this mantra while offering water to Tulsi plant.

Naivedya Mantra

ॐ प्राणाय स्वाहा । ॐ अपानाय स्वाहा ।
ॐ व्यानाय स्वाहा । ॐ उदानाय स्वाहा ।
ॐ समानाय स्वाहा । ॐ ब्रह्मणे स्वाहा । नैवेद्यं समर्पयामि ॥

· Transliteration ·

Om Praanaaya Swaahaa | Om Apaanaaya Swaahaa |
Om Vyaanaaya Swaahaa | Om Udaanaaya Swaahaa |
Om Samaanaaya Swaahaa | Om Brahmane Swaahaa |
Naivedyam Samarpayaami ||

· Meaning ·

I offer this to prana (respiratory system), I offer this to apana (excretory system), I offer this to vyana (circulatory system),
I offer this to udana (sensory system),
I offer this to samana (digestive system), I offer this to the Brahman (supreme God), I offer this Naivedya to You.

· Information ·

Naivedya is a Sanskrit word that means `offering to God'. Food is first offered to God and is called naivedya (or naivedyam) and once the food is blessed by God it is called prasad. For offering naivedya, the mantras associated with panch prana or the five vital energies (prana, apana, vyana, udana and samana) along with that for the Brahman (universal soul or the supreme God) are recited. While reciting, eyes are closed and aroma or essence of the naivedya is directed towards the deity.

PEACE

Om Asato Ma Sadgamaya

ॐ असतो मा सद्गमय ।
तमसो मा ज्योतिर्गमय ।
मृत्योर्माऽमृतं गमय ।
ॐ शान्तिः शान्तिः शान्तिः ॥

• Transliteration •

Om Asato Maa Sadgamaya |
Tamaso Maa Jyotirgamaya |
Mrutyorma-amrutam Gamaya |
Om Shaantih, Shaantih, Shaantih ||

• Meaning •

From illusions lead me to truth, from ignorance lead me to enlightenment, from death lead me to immortality. May there be peace all around.

• Information •

This mantra is also known as "pavanama" (purifying) mantra. It encourages the person reciting it to seek truth, knowledge and wisdom.

Om Sahana Vavatu

ॐ सह नाववतु ।
सह नौ भुनक्तु ।
सह वीर्यं करवावहै ।
तेजस्वि नावधीतमस्तु मा विद्विषावहै ।
ॐ शान्तिः शान्तिः शान्तिः ॥

• **Transliteration** •

Om Saha Naavavatu |
Saha Nau Bhunaktu |
Saha Viryam Karavaavahai |
Tejasvi Naavadhitamastu Maa Vidvishaavahai |
Om Shaantih Shaantih Shaantih ||

• **Meaning** •

May God protect us both, the teacher and the student,
may we work together with vigour,
may our efforts be enlightening without any hate.
May there be peace all around.

• **Information** •

Students and the teacher usually recite this mantra together at the beginning of a class, to remove any negative feelings and create harmony. This mantra occurs in the Krishna Yajurveda Taittiriya Upanishad.

Kale Varshatu Parjanyah

काले वर्षतु पर्जन्यः पृथिवी सस्यशालिनी।
देशो ऽयं क्षोभरहितः ब्राह्मणास्सन्तु निर्भयाः ॥

Transliteration

Kaale Varshatu Parjanyah Pruthvi Sasyashaalini |
Desho-Yam Kshobharahitah Braahamanaassantu Nirbhayaah ||

Meaning

May the clouds rain on time, may the earth be covered in vegetation, may there be no suffering in the country, may good people live without fear.

Information

This mantra is often recited at the end of any auspicious ritual. It prays for the entire country's well-being, and for the welfare of good people.

Om Sarve Bhavantu Sukhinah

ॐ सर्वे भवन्तु सुखिनः
सर्वे सन्तु निरामयाः ।
सर्वे भद्राणि पश्यन्तु
मा कश्चिद्दुःखभाग्भवेत् ।
ॐ शान्तिः शान्तिः शान्तिः ॥

· Transliteration ·

Om Sarve Bhavantu Sukhinah
Sarve Santu Niraamayaah |
Sarve Bhadraani Pashyantu
Maa Kaschiddukhbhaagbhavet |
Om Shaantih Shaantih Shaantih ||

· Meaning ·

May all beings be happy,
may everyone be free from illness,
May all see good in everything, may no one suffer.
May there be peace all around.

· Information ·

The essence of this prayer is that "may all beings be happy, healthy and at peace". This is a great mantra to meditate and pray for the well-being of not only people but also of animals, birds, plants, earth, and everything, living or non-living.

Om Sarvesham Swastirbhavatu

ॐ सर्वेषां स्वस्तिर्भवतु ।
सर्वेषां शान्तिर्भवतु ।
सर्वेषां पूर्णंभवतु ।
सर्वेषां मङ्गलंभवतु ।
ॐ शान्तिः शान्तिः शान्तिः ॥

Transliteration

Om Sarveshaam Swastirbhavatu |
Sarveshaam Shaantirbhavatu |
Sarveshaam Purnambhavatu |
Sarveshaam Mangalambhavatu |
Om Shaantih Shaantih Shaantih ||

Meaning

May all be well,
May there be peace in all,
May there be fulfillment in all,
May there be auspiciousness in all,
May there be peace all around.

Information

The original form of this shanti mantra is believed to occur in the Brihadaranyaka Upanishad. It is an invocation for harmony and welfare of all creations.

ॐ पूर्णमदः पूर्णमिदं पूर्णात्पूर्णमुदच्यते ।
पूर्णस्य पूर्णमादाय पूर्णमेवावशिष्यते ।
ॐ शान्तिः शान्तिः शान्तिः ॥

Transliteration

Om Purnamadah Purnamidam Purnaatpurnamudachayate |
Purnasya Purnamaadaaya Purnamevaavashishyate |
Om Shaantih Shaantih Shaantih ||

Meaning

That (God or Brahman) is complete and
this is (you or Atman are) complete. When you separate yourself
from the infinite completeness, it is still complete
(like removing a drop from the ocean, the ocean is still complete
and the drop still has all properties of the ocean).
May there be peace all around.

Information

This shanti mantra is from the Ishavasya Upanishad.
The completeness here refers to Brahman, supreme divinity,
the infinite soul of the universe or the ultimate consciousness, and
how we are all a part of it although we are separate beings.

Swasti Prajabhyah

स्वस्ति प्रजाभ्यः परिपालयन्ताम्
न्यायेन मार्गेण महीं महीषाः |
गोब्राह्मणेभ्यः शुभमस्तु नित्यम्
लोकाः समस्ताः सुखिनो भवन्तु ॥

Transliteration

Swasti Prajaabhyah Paripaalyantaam
Nyaayen Maargen Mahim Mahishaah |
Gobraahmanebhyah Shubhamastu Nityam
Lokaah Samastaah Sukhino Bhavantu ||

Meaning

May all people be well, may leaders rule the earth righteously, may the animals and wise men always be blessed with auspiciousness, may all beings be happy.

Information

This is another mantra that is often recited at the end of any auspicious rituals. Such mantras praying for global harmony and welfare are known as lokakshema (welfare) or mangala (auspicious) mantras.

JOURNAL AND NOTES

Journal

Q1. If you could meet a character from Hindu mythology, who would it be, and what questions would you ask them?

Q2. Imagine you are a character in the Ramayana. Write about your adventures and challenges.

Journal

Q3. List three qualities of Hanuman that you admire. If you had these qualities for a day, how would you use it to help others?

Q4. Choose a shloka or mantra that you like. Write about how it makes you feel and why you like it.

Journal

Q5. Imagine you are a tiny insect living on a Tulsi plant. Write about your daily adventures and observations.

Q6. Draw or describe a Hindu symbol that you find interesting. What does it represent, and why does it appeal to you?

Journal

Q7. Create your own symbol that represents something important to you.

Q8. Choose a Hindu deity and write about their qualities and attributes. How can you incorporate these qualities into your own life?

Journal

Q7. Create your own symbol that represents something important to you.

Q8. Choose a Hindu deity and write about their qualities and attributes. How can you incorporate these qualities into your own life?

Journal

Q9. Create your own mythical creature inspired by Hindu mythology. What powers and qualities would it have?

Q10. What is the concept of dharma (righteous duty) according to you? Think about how you can follow your dharma in your daily life, considering your responsibilities and actions.

Journal

Q11. Imagine going on an adventure inspired by Hindu myths. Where would you go, who would you meet and what challenges would you face?

Q12. Think of a verse or teaching from Hindu scriptures that encourages gratitude. Write about three things you are grateful for today.

Journal

Q13. Choose a Hindu festival and learn about its significance. Write about how your family celebrates this festival and what it means to you.

Q14. Based on the concept of dharma or righteous duty, what are your responsibilities and duties in your family, school, and community?

Journal

Q15. Write a new short story involving your favorite Hindu deity. What difficulties do they face, and how do they overcome them?

Notes and doodles

Notes and doodles

Notes and doodles

Notes and doodles

Notes and doodles

Notes and doodles

Notes and doodles

Notes and doodles

Notes and doodles

Notes and doodles

Notes and doodles

Notes and doodles

Notes and doodles

Notes and doodles

Notes and doodles

Notes and doodles

Notes and doodles

Notes and doodles

Notes and doodles

Notes and doodles